KNOW

Penny Stock Trading

The NO-SERIES *Presents*

KNOW

Penny Stock Trading

How to Start Trading Penny Stocks and Make Money

No-To-Know Publication

While attempts have been made to verify the information contained within this publication, neither the author nor the publisher assumes any responsibility for errors, omissions, interpretation or usage of the subject matter herein.

This publication contains the opinions and ideas of its author and is intended for informational purpose only. The author and publisher shall in no event held liable for any loss or other damages incurred from the usage of this publication.

*Note there is no guarantee that you will ever make any money at all from penny stocks, but in fact incur losses. It all depends on your level of dedication, motivation, and expertise. Penny stock trading is very risky, and you should proceed so at your own risk.

**Lastly, please be warned that this contains strong languages which some people may find harsh. If you're easily offended, proceed with caution.

ISBN 978-1-517-71796-4

Printed in the United States of America

First Edition

CONTENTS

Chapter 1

Why Bother with Penny Stock Trading

The New Gold Mine To Riches?

"Grittani had noticed shares of a company called Nutranomics, which trade over the counter under the symbol NNRX, had shot up due to what he felt was the manipulation of scammers: the stock had tripled in just a month. Last Monday, Grittani detected that the stock was losing momentum, and he felt that at the very least a small pullback was imminent. Sure enough, the stock tumbled almost 60% in the span of 23 minutes. Though he didn't benefit from the entire plunge, Grittani walked away $8,000 in ten minutes." - **CNN Money News**

Would you like to make **tens of thousands of dollars** in mere minutes? How does never working another day of your life sound to you? If you could sit at home all day and still make a better living that all your friends who have 9-5 daytime desk jobs...would you do it?

Okay, these things definitely sound too good to be true. *The fact is*, they are **perfectly plausible.**

You could very well work the type of "job" that requires nothing more than a small fund of starting money, research, and internet access.

The only downside is that you'll be expected to take risks if you want to reap benefits. You won't ever be able to get something for nothing, but trading stocks is pretty damn close.

For the amount of effort required, playing the stock market has a surprisingly high reward.

How much reward are we talking, exactly?

At the very top of the list, **Warren Buffett** reigns supreme as a penny stock and day trading investor. Last year he brought in $13.5 billion.

Just to put that into perspective, let's say that you brought in $30,000 last year. This means that Warren Buffett wheeled and dealed so effectively that he was earning your yearly salary every 1.2 minutes.

On the other side of the coin, there exist thousands of stories like that of **Jeff Rose**, a well-known financial blogger. Rose made a bad choice and lost $5,000 instantaneously after investing in a penny stock. He bought shares for twice what they were actually worth, other people sold their shares, and the stock took a nosedive...all in a matter of seconds.

Scared yet?

The bottom line is that there is no “average salary” for a penny stock investor for there is such a vast gulf between

potential and **missed return** that penny stocks are often compared to slot machines and grab bags.

Return is a fancy word for the cold, hard cash that you could be receiving by *trading penny stocks* right at this very moment.

Are Penny Stocks Good Investments?

So why aren't you delving into the world of economy and payout?

- Possibly, you might be a little strapped for cash.
- Maybe you don't know enough about the stock market to even justify tossing in money that you consider expendable.
- Or maybe, you've heard that penny stocks are a poor investment choice. (Or let's be completely honest here and admit that you might not even know what a "**penny stock**" actually is. It's cool.)

The stock market is an ever-changing, economy-driven hub for all businesses and their respective stocks.

Every Wall Street scene of every movie you've ever watched is true - the stock market's physical face is just a bunch of crazed salary men running around with algorithms and complicated spreadsheets. But under the surface, the stock market is actually just a bunch of scared, business-minded risk takers with too much money for their own good.

In a world of huge investors and stocks that can reach a value of over $700 for a single share, where do you fit in? How does the little guy catch a big break?

The Benefits Of Penny Stocks

Before it was a popular energy drink brand, **Monster** was once a player in the penny stock market. Shares that sold for less than $5 each have now hit a return high of over 1000%, and that's nothing to sneeze at.

Everyday people just like you are making a fortune on trading penny stocks, even at this exact moment.

What have you heard about penny stocks?

Most likely, you've heard that **A)** they are a cheap, easy way to start investing, **B)** they are less likely than traditional stocks to bring in large amounts of revenue, and **C)** they are significantly riskier.

To some extent, all of these are true.

If you're concerned about the amount of money you have to toss around, penny stocks are the perfect way to explore investing without sinking your entire savings. However, don't confuse "cheap" with "easy."

Penny stock traders must have a firm working knowledge of the internet, the general economy and current political and social happenings, and an understanding of whatever software they are using to decipher data.

(You will have to sit at your computer all day to be ready for market changes at a moment's notice, and you'll have to be smart enough to accurately predict those changes.)

Since many penny stocks are not regulated or held to market standards, they can sink quickly without warning. In a market where even the slightest nuance is can make or break you, yes, the risk is higher.

Big Fish In Small Pond Equals Money

"In case you didn't know, just about everyone in finance hates on penny stocks as too risky, manipulated, illegal, unethical, scummy, beneath them - every negative adjective you can think of. And yet somehow I've always made six figures/year trading them. As I tell anyone who will listen, that all the manipulation and sketchiness is just part of the game…the good news is that's it's a VERY predictable game." - **Timothy Sykes**, self-made multi-millionaire

If the risk is higher, are the rewards more tantalizing?

It depends on how successful you are at making insightful choices. (And a little luck wouldn't hurt, either.)

Remember that most giants of the **regular stock market** are professional accountants and financial firms...not everyday people such as yourself. In that dog eat dog world, even internet lag of 1 millisecond in buy/sell communication can mean bankruptcy.

The fact is, making money in the traditional stock market is an explosive, aggressive game that will 9 times out of 10 have a larger impact on your revenue.

Unfortunately, running in that league is nearly impossible.

If you are truly looking to start a portfolio and have personal control over what investments you make, **penny stock trading** *is more accessible.*

How much money would you make trying to force your way into Wall Street?

Sometimes being a big fish in a little pond can be much more rewarding.

No Risk. No Reward.

So there you have it...

Penny stocks are risky, without a doubt, but they can lead to the kind of riches you've only dreamed of.

If you want to know how to vacation in the Caribbean and drive a Ferrari on the weekends, read on.

Millionaires like **Timothy Sykes** swear that with a little intelligence and gumption, your salary can be downright huge.

Do you have what it takes? Do you want to know exactly what to do in order to get started and bring in a year's worth of salary in a matter of hours?

Chapter 2

Catching Up to Speed with the Fundamentals

Are You Caught Up To Speed?

If someone asked you to define "**over the counter**" stocks, would you know how to respond? What if someone asked you the precise location of Wall Street?

If you're feeling uncomfortable *(or at the very least, a little less confident)*, then how about a quick lesson in stock market jargon?

Thankfully, you can fix nearly all of those issues easily.

How The Stocks Work

First, let's break down what penny stocks actually are.

To understand them, you'll need to know how stocks work, in general.

In simplest terms, investing in a **stock** is a *way to financially back a certain company.*

By buying "pieces" of the company in the form of stock shares, you technically own a part of the business.

Stockholders can buy one share or hundreds, depending on how far they want to go to support their chosen company. Buying stocks is a way to invest your money in a company to help it flourish, or simply keep it afloat.

(Think of this like giving your niece or nephew money for their graduation. They might squander it on bad decisions, or they might use it for college and grow to be a successful, responsible adult. But whatever the outcome, you threw in your lot.)

Penny Stock Trading vs. Regular Stock Trading

Are penny stocks the new gold mine to riches? It's a nice sentiment, but can it be true for you?

Penny stocks are just like regular stocks, except *they trade for less than $5 per share* (some people define it as less than $3 per share).

To put that into layman's terms - you can purchase a surprising amount of penny stock shares for the same amount you would spend to buy just a few shares of a stock market heave-hitter.

Of course, there are other nuances that define what exactly a penny stock is (some are not regulated according to market standards, etc.), but the price tag is really the deciding factor.

Millionaires like self-made Timothy Sykes will tell you that you can learn the patterns of penny stock trading and become successful nearly instantaneously. It's impossible to predict or guarantee exactly how a stock will rise or fall, but you can't argue with quantifiable evidence.

Understand The Stock Market

While you might have appreciated the earlier stock market lesson quickie, there is quite a lot more that you should know before delving in.

First of all, where is the stock market?

If you answered London or New York City, you're partially right, but also very, very wrong.

The stock market is technically NOT a thing or a place at all; but rather, a meeting of **supply and demand**. Specifically, a meeting of the money behind and produced by supply and demand.

- The **New York Stock Exchange**, famous for weeping investors and shouting stock brokers, is one place where the stock market takes on physical form. At this kind of facility, investors can make oral or digital bids on stocks.

- **NASDAQ**, on the other hand, is an example of a digital stock world. The same kinds of transactions are made, but there is simply a lot less shouting and need for recycling thousands of sales forms every day. (NASDAQ is an environmentalist's wet dream.)

If you're picturing a giant conglomeration of greedy businessmen, companies desperate to stay afloat, corporate giants making money hand over fist, and your own Roth IRA money being tossed around, you have a solid grasp on the truth of the stock market.

What Is A Penny Stock?

Now, let's talk about what penny stocks are. Penny stocks are not your run of the mill stock market companies, and they certainly aren't regulated the same as the big box stores and genius companies that NASDAQ and Wall Street toss around.

The **Securities and Exchange Commission (SEC)**, keeps a list of every company open for stock trading on the market. While penny stocks are required to register, they are not held to the same regulations as other stocks that don't trade through pink sheets.

Which brings us to our next thrilling item on the agenda - **Over the Counter (OTC)** stocks. An OTC stock is one that is posted on the **Over The Counter Bulletin Board (OTCBB)**. Stocks that are posted on this "board" are not currently trading at levels like Microsoft or Disney, but they are still being regulated and accounted for.

You will find some penny stocks at this level, and they are generally much safer than **Pink Sheet stocks**. Pink Sheets are at the very bottom of the trading totem pole. Bankrupt, unwilling to share financial information with the public, or trading at such small levels that they literally cannot meet basic stock financial requirements to be considered a "company," these stocks are incredibly risky.

And wouldn't you know it, many penny stocks are traded on this black market of the stock world. They aren't illegal, but they certainly aren't to be trusted unconditionally. But like anything with a little bite, you can stand to make a rather grandiose profit investing in Pink Sheet stocks.

Nestle, the corporate giant from Switzerland with mouth-watering chocolate and even more appetizing sales, is famous for trading in Pink Sheets because it gives them more wiggle room concerning rules and regulations.

The Dark Side Of The Penny

"The real question is this: was all this legal? Absolutely fucking not. But we were making more money than we knew what do with." - **Jordan Belfort,** The Wolf of Wall Street

Concerned about the rules behind **penny stock** and **Pink Sheet trading?**

There are two simple rules that can save you from disaster nearly every time: do your research, and don't trust anyone. And since research can only get you so far, the most important of these two rules is clearly the latter.

No one, not your investment agent, CNN, or even your own mother, is going to give you the god honest truth when it comes to investing.

Why? Because everyone who plays in the stock market is in it to win it.

Stupid people don't invest in stocks. Clever people who know how to motivate and manipulate others do.

If you want to come out on top, you have to keep your wits about you, not get bogged down by greed, and realize that there is no such thing as a free lunch. If you have to question whether something is legal or not, it isn't worth your time.

Questionable stock market activities include but are not limited to: "**pumping and dumping,**" (talking up a stock until buyers swarm, then selling for increased profits), investing in stocks under a name that is not your own without permission, cheating on taxes, taking or giving insider stock tips, or investing in a fraudulent company.

A Cautionary Tale

You should obviously be conscious to not actually do any of these things, but also be aware that there are people who make a livelihood off cheating beginner investors just like yourself.

Pump and dump stock schemes are incredibly common, and it's very likely that you'll run into someone hyping up a bad stock or company during your first month as a penny stock investor.

Don't take the bait, and don't be tempted to play the game yourself. People have been investigated by the IRS for far less.

With penny stocks, you skip the middle man. By investing in penny stocks, you tell the company that you will be the one to work and invest for a return. Sometimes it works, and something it crashes and burns.

The essence of penny stocks is profit in return for self-reliance.

In the wise words of Jordan Belfort from The Wolf of Wall Street, *"Let me tell you something. There's no nobility in poverty. I've been a poor man, and I've been a rich man. And I choose rich every fucking time."*

Chapter 3

Research! Research! Research!

Anybody Can Do It

"You don't need to be a rocket scientist. Investing is not a game where the guy with the 160 IQ beats the guy with 130 IQ." - **Warren Buffet**

Young or old, inexperienced or not, you can start trading stocks with very little initial effort. In fact, as long as you're 21 years of age *(18 in some states)*, you can get involved in penny stock trading anytime you want.

The very first thing you'll want to do is begin researching penny stocks and find one that appeals to you.

How To Get Started

Many stock specialists and investors will recommend that you try out some normal, mid-cap stocks first. The goal from this little excursion into investing is to learn how to organize and balance your finances.

In addition, you'll need to learn what essential documents (like *income statements* and *cash flow statements*) are and how to read them. If you already have experience with the stuffy business side of things, then you're ready to delve into research.

First things first!

Learn the difference between **hearsay** and **quantifiable evidence** of stock happenings. And once you have that down, realize that not every site advertising honesty and publishing exact stock numbers is telling you the truth.

Got it?

Where To Research

Now it's time to use both kinds of stock information to pinpoint penny stocks that will be a perfect fit for your portfolio.

- Megasites like AllPennyStocks.com and PennyStockList.com will give you the latest stock rises and collapses.

- If you want to listen to tips and rumors, subscribe to a few newsletters or visit the various penny stock sub-reddits on Reddit.com, where investors are constantly swapping advice and hints.

- Remember that you can always check out sites like Investopedia.com and NASDAQ.com if you feel like reading more how-to information along the way.

Determine Your Stocks

"Economics is all about consumption. People either spend money now or they use financial instruments - like bonds, stocks and savings accounts - so they can spend more later." - **Adam Davidson**

"Successful investing is anticipating the anticipations of others." - **John Maynard Keynes**

If the stock market is so incredibly risky (and penny stocks are even more volatile), then how will you know what to invest in?

Start with this simple idea: stocks are a reflection of what consumers want.

If Nike suddenly releases a brand new, innovative shoe design, you can bet that their stocks are going to skyrocket.

Here's a more in-depth example. **AMD** and **Intel** are notorious for releasing similar computer processors at roughly the same time every two years or so. (They have a cold-war style marketing competition.)

So in the instance, here is what you do:

1.) **Do some research.** How often are new processors released?

2.) **Wait until the lowest point of the cycle.** It's been a while since something was released, and you still have another 6 months minimum before anything big hits the market.

3.) **Buy stock from your preferred company.**

4.) **Watch the news concerning your company.** When your company releases their new processor, be ready!

5.) **Sell your stock!**

What Stocks To Look For

This kind of investing is fairly straightforward and easy to research because big name companies are eager to market their upcoming products. Of course, this is because they want a lot of stock investors...but their greed can also play to your advantage.

- The technology market is one of the simplest areas to invest in, simply because of hyped up advertising campaigns. (You can also play this game with *AMD* vs. *Nvidia* graphics cards, *Macbooks* vs. *laptops*, and eventually even currently-private companies like *FitBit* and *Jawbone.*)

So how do you apply these tactics to penny stocks, where the companies are oftentimes secretive or too small to have a marketing campaign to follow?

Remember the initial rule - the economy is *based off of consumer demand.*

You don't have to know exactly what a penny stock company is selling, but you can still have a general idea of how marketable they are.

For example, let's say you are thinking about investing in a company that ships oranges from some wonderfully tropical company to the States. The trick is to think out of the box.

- Are the oranges organically grown? There is a huge demand for "health food" in the US at the moment. Pay attention to trends, because they will have a definite impact on imports.

- Take a gander at the prospected orange harvest for Florida and Georgia. If the weather has been poor this year, there will be a higher demand for imported oranges.

- Are there any current health trends going on that would impact how many oranges will sell in stores? For example, investing in a company that imported Acai berries during the Acai health craze would have made you a very rich person. Similarly, avocados are still "big" in the foodie world, and are predictably doing very well.

What Stock Sectors To Avoid

In general, you'll want to stay away from agricultural, mining, and specific medical stocks.

Think about medicines like *Accutane* (commonly used to treat cases of severe cystic acne) and *Yaz* (a birth control pill). These medicines have undergone massive recalls and large lawsuits have been filed due to their outstandingly bad side effects.

What does that mean?

If they had stocks at one point, they definitely don't have anything left now!

So the trick here is to invest in new **medical technology**, but *NOT* in specific medications. The more specific a product is, the greater a chance there is for it to fail or be made obsolete in the near future.

- When you invest, *go vague*. Think about everything in terms of innovative potential, not in terms of how useful a particular product will be. Long-term wins the investment game.

So the idea behind all of this is: do your research.

Investing in a tiny company with little to no marketing pizazz can be dangerous, but your intelligence can offset the risk.

Watch for companies that have gone bankrupt in the past, and don't let anyone talk you into buying before you've gathered as much information as possible. And overall, try investing in stocks that reflect **ideas** *more* than **actual products**.

Penny stocks move fast, but you need to combine speed with thought if you want to make any money.

Tools To Get

"The human brain has 100 billion neurons, each neuron connected to 10 thousand other neurons. Sitting on your shoulders is the most complicated object in the known universe." - **Michio Kaku**

Okay, the human brain is great...but do you know what's even better?

Software. Powerful, efficient software.

Tool #1 - Before you do anything else, you need to acquire a copy of some sort of spreadsheet-style software. If you want to follow the example of *90%* of the stock magicians of today, you will want to use something like **Microsoft Excel** to keep track of your earnings and losses. (Looking for something free? **Open Office** is a very similar set of office software tools that will get the basic job done.)

Tool #2 - After you've laid the foundation, you'll want to run a program that can give you stock alerts, accurate trading numbers, and information from brokers. Timothy Sykes, famous for making millions at a very young age through trading penny stocks, has used **Realtick** since 1997. (Realtick has been around for far longer - 25 years!)

Tool #3 - If you're looking for software that can provide newsletters and alerts, **Profiding** is another possibility.

Tool #4 - Finally, **Eye in the Sky Trade Planning** rounds out Sykes' top three trading software programs. Eye is mostly used for finding stocks that fit your investment requirements. (You can use it to search by price, return, size of the company, *etc.*)

Task: Do The Perquisites

If you're feeling a bit overwhelmed, take a step back...and remind yourself that penny stocks can make the average person rich as a sultan.

Do you want to be rich? Of course you do, or you wouldn't be reading this!

Here's are the steps to take, right now:

<u>STEP 1</u>: Download or buy a spreadsheet-based program to track your earnings/losses.

<u>STEP 2</u>: Subscribe to every trading newsletter, site, and forum you can get your hands.

<u>STEP 3</u>: Use an email or google account separate from your personal account to subscribe to said services.

<u>STEP 4</u>: Invest in at least one good stock trading software program, like Realtick.

<u>STEP 5</u>: Read a summary (from five different sites) of the biggest, best-selling penny stocks of the previous year.

<u>STEP 6</u>: Turn on that investing software and get to know the interface.

<u>STEP 7</u>: Make a list of specific investing areas that interest you (medical, technology, oil, etc.).

Chapter 4

Doing It Yourself

Learn As You Go

"Greed, for lack of a better word, is good. Greed is right. Greed works. Greed clarifies and cuts through to the essence of the evolutionary spirit." - **Gordon Gekko,** Wall Street

Let's assume that you are, in fact, greedy. *Welcome to being human!*

So what is the best way to assure you turn the ultimate profit with stocks?

Although it basically means you'll always be on thin ice when it comes to investing, the single most important thing you can do is *cut out the middle man*. Don't rely on someone to do research that you could be doing yourself.

If you are intelligent enough to put away money to invest in the first place, then you should have the smarts necessary for choosing a stock.

Here's the rule for using a broker: **time is money**.

- If you think your time is worth more than what you would be paying someone to hunt down stocks for you, then hire a middle man.

- If you're able to do the legwork on your own, then by all means, go it alone!

Without a broker, this entire process is going to get a lot more interesting.

True, you're going to skip paying a lot of useless fees. But are you ready to put in the amount of effort needed to control you own portfolio?

If your answer is a confident "**yes!**" then you're ready to learn about the software that will let you take charge of your own investments.

Task: Start Trading Now

For the steps below, you'll want to download a free trial of the program E-Trade. Another useful online source is TD Ameritrade.

1.) Open your program and bring up your *"Menu"* box.

2.) Sync your menu with the *"Call"* box. (When you click on a stock in the menu, the Call box should give you detailed information about whatever you have selected. Look for the *"Link"* button in the top right corner of each tool for this option.)

3.) Scroll over and assign your second page of menus as follows: One 3-minute updated chart, one 15-minute updated chart, and a daily overall chart. (You can make charts by selecting *"Charts"* under the main *"Tools"* tab.)

4.) Adjust and drag menus to you screen size, keeping in mind that you have various pages to work with.

5.) Make a third page for scanners. (Make some scanners by choosing *"Strategy Scanner"* under the *"Tools"* tab. Assign whatever options you prefer. (You can specifically target what stocks hit a new high by specifying price limitations.)

6.) At the top right of every tool on this third page, choose *"Settings"* from the dropdown menu and filter stocks by price. This ensures that only penny stocks will show on these charts, even if your portfolio contains larger holdings.

7.) Use the *"Tools"* tab to stretch you screen horizontally and vertically. (This will give you plenty of room for charts and menus.)

8.) To actually buy a stock, you can create a **Regular Order** or a **Spread Order** by entering the sale into the bottom of the **Call** box tool.

9.) Pull up an **Order Status** box. (You can find it under the *"Tools"* tab.) **E-Trade** is notorious for slow buy and sale notifications, so this particular tool is highly recommended.

10.) Sell stocks with the same order fields in the bottom of the **Call** box.

How To Choose Your Stocks Yourself

Now that you know how to use the software, how will you choose what stocks to buy?

To meet your maximum earning potential, you must minimize risk. *"This is the penny stock market!"* you say, *"There is no way to minimize risk!"*

While you would be correct in terms of realistic expectations, there are proven ways to avoid treading thin ice when you invest.

Here are some general tips to follow if you want to "**Do It Yourself**":

1.) Understand that the stock market is surrounded by a dense layer of *social manipulation*. Every source you find online is a player in this game. If you ignored the advice from earlier and are still subscribed to sources like stock newsletters, don't let your extracurricular reading affect your tactics. Instead, let it season your understanding of the symbiotic relationship between **media** and **stocks**.

2.) Don't make extensive research projects on one particular stock. Penny stocks are in and out, one and done. Penny stock companies are also often *underpublicized*. By the time they hit the news, you've already missed your chance.

3.) Use **charts** to map *highs* and *lows*. You should have charts that update every few minutes, every fifteen minutes to half an hour, and charts that update daily. Pay attention to what sells.

4.) *Watch* the **news**. Get acquainted with trends, popular science, and gadgetry. The more you know, the more you'll make.

How To Think About The Stocks

Don't be afraid to rely on **common sense** and *ignore your gut feeling*. Save that gut feeling for love and choosing a team in fantasy football.

Here's an example:

You see on **Yahoo! Mail** and the Reddit.com/r/pennystocks that a company called **Wiznits**, a company specializing in alpaca sweaters, is currently selling stocks for $1.21 a share. (Unless you're gullible or a stocks newbie...until you're able to tell a sham from the real deal, stay out of the affiliated stock news!)

Reading further, you see that these popular websites are praising Wiznits for quickly rising in popularity and value. It is currently February, and the winter in the US has been unusually warm.

Here is what your thought process should be like:

- **1 second** - realize that Wiznits is already featured on huge, popular websites. This probably means that Wiznits is currently at its peak sale point, and can only decrease from here.

- **10 seconds** - using your buying software, pull up a chart depicting Wiznits' stock value over the last months and confirm your theory.

- **1 second** - reflect on the fact that it is now February and the demand for alpaca sweaters is going to decrease drastically now that people are no longer searching for holiday gifts, and instead looking forward to spring apparel.

So in less than a minute, you can make an informed decision concerning whether or not you should invest in any given company.

How To Make Money Off Your Stocks

"One of the funny things about the stock market is that every time one person buys, another sells, and both think they are astute." - **William Feather**

When you were in school, did you memorize the facts just to get by, or did you understand things like calculus and photosynthesis on a conceptual level?

If you weren't a **conceptual learner** back then...you need to become one now.

While you can mostly rely on cold, hard facts for purchasing stock shares, selling shares will demand that you make

assumptions and **guesses** about the future state of the economy.

No, you aren't just speculating about one company anymore...you are literally making predictions about what supply and demand will be in the near future. And of course, supply and demand for your chosen stock will involve a hundred other factors that seem to have nothing to do with your stock...on the surface.

Think of this like playing poker. You'll need to discard cards (stocks) in order to win the pot, but first you need to decide which cards to toss. *Aces? Sevens? Queens?* How does one decide which cards, or stocks, to discard?

- Use **keywords** and **Ctrl+F** to quick search for your stocks in current news. If the media gets ahold of your company, you're either doing very well (and you'll know), or the stock has peaked. *Sell.*

- Use the same researching techniques to keep an eye on things like **legal battles** and **recalls**. Any company can have a falling out. Be ready to sell at the drop of a hat. *(GM, Exxon, etc.)*

- Don't make statements like, *"I'll sell at $3 and no less."* Not every penny stock is going to increase to $3. Putting **selling requirements** is *limiting the selling potential* of your investment.

- **Sell** if you *make a mistake.* If you invest in a stock that tanks, own up to your mistake and sell.

Do You Really Want To Go At It Alone?

"For twenty dollars I can tell you a lot of things. For thirty dollars I can tell you more. And for fifty dollars I can tell you everything."
- Pee-Wee's Big Adventure (1985)

Yes, trading stocks on your own is much more technical and confusing.

Thankfully, there are dozens of resources available, and most companies that publish stock software also provide free support.

(Mind you, no one is going to hold your hand when you have to decide what stocks to buy. E-Trade employees can help you alter the color of your daily stock charts, but they aren't even going to advise you to choose one stock over another.)

Really, deciding whether or not to use a penny stock broker is up to you.

Do you want to pay that hypothetical *"thirty dollars"* for someone to tell you more about investing, or do you want to pay nothing and find out for yourself?

If you have the time and the patience, you have what it takes to make your own way in the stock market.

Chapter 5

Getting A Broker

Helping Hands

Not ready to go at it alone when it comes to investing in penny stocks? **That's fine.**

You can shell out a small percent of your earnings to someone called a broker. Think of a broker like you would an adult version of your high school guidance counselor.

A **good broker** will inform you of your options, potential, and resources. You and the broker can then work together to figure out a portfolio tailored for you that maximizes your potential to gather return. *Or better yet*, you can give your broker a general feel for how risky you like your endeavors, and they will make all the important decisions for you.

Tempted yet?

How To Choose A Broker

What are some **qualities** a penny stock expert will have?

While a penny stock broker will share many tendencies and traits with a traditional stock broker, there are a few differences. You should look for someone who is:

1.) **Greedy**. Penny stock brokers usually work for a percentage of your earnings. You would think that someone whose world revolves around money would be a bad thing...but when a broker's profit relies on your own, you can rest easy.

2.) **Tenacious**. Your broker needs to be like a dog with a bone when it comes to investigating companies, especially if you plan on dealing with pink sheet stocks.

3.) **Aggressive**. Some decisions have to be made with little or no information or warning. There is no room for wishy-washy behavior here.

4.) **Intelligent**. Your investment specialist should have a good grip on the economy, current news, and trending companies *and/or* products.

5.) **Honest**. Okay, so your chances of finding a completely honest broker are about the same as finding an honest lawyer. What you're looking for is someone who you can trust...to a reasonable extent, *at least!*

You're a busy person, and you don't have time to sift through the latest penny stock goings-on, much less the qualifications of specific brokers.

If you do a search for where to find a good broker, you'll instantly see companies like **OptionsXpress** and **Charles Schwab**. These options are the big box stores of the penny stock broker pool.

You'll have decent investing options and information, but it will be very sterile. (Meaning that these people probably won't invest your money in anything radical or new.)

While this is safer, it can also mean a lot of *missed opportunities*. However, brokers like these are very beginner-friendly and meant to save you time.

How To Work With Your Broker

If you're going to invest in OptionsXpress, you need to first decide how risky you want to be when playing the market.

Take **short selling**, for example. You can't play the short selling game with a broker from OptionsXpress, but you could if you were with Charles Schwab (*ironically*, the parent company of Options).

Short selling is essentially "**borrowing**" a stock and profiting when it decreases in value.

How in the world does that work, you ask? Here's how:

1.) You have a *(totally legal and not insider-leaked)* hunch that a certain stock is about to go down in value.

2.) You contact a broker and request to short sell this stock.

3.) The broker hunts down someone who owns the stock and "lends" it to you.

4.) The stock's value decreases *(just as you suspected!)*.

5.) You return the stock to the broker.

6.) The stock is sold at the price you borrowed it for *(higher)*, when it is actually worth the current value *(lower)*.

7.) You keep the difference *(after paying a small broker's fee)*.

So what does OptionsXpress have, if you can't swindle people through short sales?

It has an interactive website and desktop application, along with great brokerage contact hours.

Want to do a bit of trading on a Saturday? That's no problem also, because these brokers work weekends!

Task: Test The Water First

Continuing along the broker-friendly path, here is how you can begin trading stocks using online software from OptionsXpress (users of Charles Schwab and other companies will find this advice generally acceptable to use for their own online endeavors, notwithstanding any specific software advice).

Here's your homework:

Because you start tossing around real money, try out **Virtual Trade**, which will give you $25,000 in monopoly money and a fake market to invest it in.

You can access Virtual Trade *through* OptionsXpress' website. Try this:

1.) Create a Virtual Trade account.

2.) Select your price range, type in a stock Symbol, or search by type to find stocks to "buy."

3.) Use your virtual $25,000 to begin buying and trading stocks.

4.) Use the charts and tickers to watch stock highs and lows.

5.) Sell your stocks for a profit.

Feeling comfortable with the intricacies of the stock market yet?

Having a broker to help you feel out future investments is the key to having confidence while making decisions to support your future. *Simply put?* Keep your shirt on. These guys are professionals.

<u>Task</u>: Test Another Pond

If you found Virtual Trade to be useful and are still interested in using software from the OptionsXpress team, then try these other tools:

1.) See what other investors have up their sleeves by using the *"Idea Tool"* Trading Patterns.

2.) Use **Idea Hub** to compare trades, specifying how aggressive you want to be with investing and how much return you expect.

3.) Make an account on **oX Social** and start chatting with other investors to get tips.

4.) Use **Chains** to view real-time values of different stocks and view predicted revenue outcomes.

5.) Start placing orders on **All-In-One Trade Ticket.**

6.) Use the **Trade and Probability Calculator** to see if your investments are worth it.

7.) Research the history of stocks on **Volatility View** *(for up to 12 months).*

If all of that still sounds like too much work...then perhaps you should consider talking with a financial counselor about investing in a mutual fund, Roth IRA, or savings account *(with a decent interest rate)* instead.

Trading stocks takes work and brains. Even hiring a very hands-on broker will still leave you with the responsibility of making large decisions.

"A consultant is someone who saves his client almost enough to pay his fee." - **Arnold H. Glasow**

The Costs Of Brokerage

With a middle man comes many hidden fees and surcharges. The thing you will have to decide, as a customer and investor, is how much your time is worth.

Are you willing to pay someone to do your research and legwork for you? What about paying someone a fee every time you buy over let's say $1,000 in shares? How do you feel about paying your company a fee depending on how often you trade?

Here are the things you should be looking for:

- **Charges per Transaction** - Every time you buy or sell, you could potentially be charged. Usually companies assign a percentage amount, which may or may not increase without warning unpredictably.

- **Trading Frequency Fees** - Are you thinking about making penny stock trading your future career? If you think you'll have a high volume of trades per day *(or even hour!)* then you might want to keep an eye out for this one.

- **Large Orders** - *Again*, this is a valid concern for people who are looking to make penny stock trading a huge part of their financial life. If you're looking at buying hundreds of shares at a time or tossing over a grand in the pot at a moment's notice, then beware these large order fees.

- **Maintenance Fees** - What maintenance could an online brokerage office possibly have? While you might call bull on this fee the same way you would for a bank's "*processing fee*," that doesn't mean that you won't get charged for it.

- **Minimum Order Charges** - Easily one of the largest *(and therefore we can unabashedly call it more irritating)* fees, minimum order charges are the number one fee you should attempt to avoid. The more you spend in order to buy new shares, the more you'll have to expect from those shares when you sell them back. Remember the idea that planning to sell a stock for a certain amount is "limiting" the stock, because it might not ever hit that number? Minimum order charges can force your hand by adding value to a stock that it doesn't actually have.

Is Brokerage Right For You?

The bottom line? Read the fine print.

If you still don't get it or are in doubt, contact the help desk at whatever company you're interested in and ask blunt questions.

Make sure to take screenshots of whatever conversation you have, *(or even better, conduct it through email)*, so that you'll have a record of whatever you were promised.

There's no harm in protecting yourself or having a healthy bit of paranoia. It might even keep you from getting into a financially tight spot in the future!

Here is *what you can do* to get ready and find a broker:

1.) Research companies

2.) Grill customer help representatives for information on hidden fees.

3.) Use Virtual Trade and toss around that $25,000.

4.) Sign up with whatever site you've chosen.

5.) Contact a broker or use their software to start buying and selling.

Chapter 6

Becoming A Broker Yourself

From Amateur To Professional

"How many millionaires do you know who have become wealthy by investing in savings accounts? I rest my case." - **Robert G. Allen**

A few months or years have passed, and you've gained a respectable amount of knowledge *(and presumably, wealth)* from investing.

Maybe you've established dominance over other investors by being constantly referred to. Maybe you have the Midas touch when it comes to selecting stocks for your portfolio.

Whatever you've done, you're feeling confident.

How would you feel about taking things to the next level? How would you like to make more money with less effort?

Task: Test Yourself

First, let's take a test. Answer the questions below truthfully:

1.) You make a bad investment and realize that the stock is only going to keep sinking. You:

a. Cut your losses and sell the investment immediately.

b. Run to your network and encourage others to invest in your stock so that the numbers will go back up.

c. Keep the stock. It might go back up someday.

2.) Your friend asks you for your opinion on a stock that is big-hitting, stable, and very expensive. This friend only has enough money to invest in a few shares of the stock. What do you say?

a. Tell your friend that he or she could buy hundreds of shares in a penny stock for the same price.

b. Encourage your friend to purchase a few shares of the stock.

c. Find a mid-range stock for them to invest in instead.

3.) A new market-tracking software comes out. Do you try it?

a. Yes, but I check it against the software I am currently using.

b. No. My current software works fine so why would I switch?

c. Yes, because it is rumored to offer market changes a few milliseconds faster than my previous software.

Are You Ready To Be A Broker Yourself?

Ready to affirm what a great broker you would be? Here are the correct answers to the questions:

1.) A is the correct answer. You would not hold onto the stock because the penny stock market is too volatile to hold out hope for a long term raise in value. And remember, publicizing false information about a tanking stock in order to sell your shares at a higher price is called "**pumping and dumping.**" *Sound illegal?* That's because it is.

2.) If your friend has a limited budget and not much marketing experience, you should guide them towards a mid-range stock that will be stable but not cost them an arm and a leg. They don't have the know-how to deal with penny stocks, and buying a handful of shares in a huge company like Apple or Wal-Mart is not going to win them much return, in the long run.

3.) A stock broker should be up-to-date with new software. You need to be on the lookout for things that could make your job easier and your sales bigger. But don't forget - there are a lot of players in the software market, but only a select handful that are actually worth your time.

So, let's assume that you answered these things right. You have a solid foundation when it comes to market knowledge, you have a healthy portion of common sense, and you know how to stay out of legal trouble.

To be honest, those are qualities that just about anyone could have.

The real trick to being a stockbroker is realizing that you hold other people's money in your hands. You are literally managing someone's livelihood. It's intimidating to think that you could financially ruin someone by miscalculating a risk or making a bad trade.

In the end, being a successful stock broker is about having the courage to take risks that are not even your own.

Becoming The Ideal Broker

"The easiest way to make money is to create something of such value that everybody wants it...the money comes automatically." - **Jordan Belfort**

What does everybody want?

People want to be told that they can make money without lifting a finger. They want it fast and they want it now.

If you, as a broker, can market a solution for their greed, then people will flock to you in droves and throw their money at your feet.

The first step to becoming a god among brokers is to convince your potential clients that your services are worth it.

Realistically, the best way to impress a client or future employer is by showing off your skills or education, just like you would for any other profession.

Getting A Broker Position At Firm

While any college degree will be helpful, a degree in **business** or **accounting** will be the most impressive.

Similarly, consider getting registered as a **CPA** *(certified public accountant)* if you are serious about a career as a stock broker. (Being a CPA is especially handy if you have any interest in investing for groups of people or businesses versus investing on behalf of individuals.)

Straight from the handy site TotalJobs.com, here is a list of necessary skills you will need to have if you want to work for a **brokerage firm:**

- Handling customers over the phone
- Writing and formatting letters and emails
- Paperwork filing
- Attending meetings
- General account handling
- Researching new technology and market statistics

This list is based on an entry-level, assistant broker position.

Being an experienced broker with assistants of your own will mean even longer hours, excellent customer service and communication skills, and the ability to make quick decisions on your own.

What Type Of Broker You Want To Be?

"You can't be a good value investor without being an independent thinker - you're seeing valuations that the market is not appreciating. But it's critical that you understand why the market isn't seeing the value you do." - **Joe Greenblatt**

As far as types of brokers go, there are three categories you need to choose from.

- First of all, there are **bank brokers**. Specializing in *safe investments* and things like *personal savings accounts*, these brokers do not deal in opinions or advice. If you are searching for a broker job that doesn't require you to know every in and out of the stock market, this is the job for you. Instead, you'll be explaining the differences between "moderate" and "aggressive" investing plans for their Roth IRA accounts. Most bank brokers are salaried, and some are even hired by companies to handle group investment plans or retirement funds.

- The second kind of broker is a **discount broker**. Likely the path you will follow if you wish *to assist clients with* *trading penny stocks*, being a discount broker means a salary but generally no commission. Discount brokers can also be called upon for questions about things like savings accounts and rollovers, so they usually have a broad spectrum of financial knowledge. If you do not possess a degree in business or accounting, this is the type for you.

- On the other hand, if your education is a vital part of your resume, then you would do well to consider being a **full-service broker**. In simple terms, this is the *crème-de-la-crème of the profession*. Full-service brokers are usually paid to attend on the job training, and then set loose to wander the wilds of investing for commission. (Working on commission means that you are paid a percentage of every sale you make, or that your salary depends on how well the company is doing as a whole.) Brokers in this field will likely deal with more traditional, main market stocks.

Companies To Apply For

Here are some companies you can apply for, today! (Arranged by review, as rated on a *1-5 star scale* by Brokerage-Review.com)

- **Charles Schwab (****)**
- **TD Ameritrade (****)**
- **Etrade (****)**
- **Fidelity Investments (****)**
- **Optionshouse (****)**
- **Thinkorswim (****)**
- **TradeMonster (****)**
- **OptionsXpress (*****)**
- **Scotttrade (*****)**

- **TradeKing** (*****)

You'll notice that the last three have *five stars*. Most of these firms require a payment per month of *less than $10*, and many of them have a $0 initial investment requirement.

With prices these cheap, how do the firms possibly afford to pay you, the employee? The answer lies in **commissions** or **sneaky hidden fees**.

As previously discussed, all major investing companies have costly tricks up their sleeves. Your clients might get hit by transaction fees, maintenance fees, or even processing fees! Congratulations though, because these fees are part of what will feed your paycheck.

Good think they're all noted in the fine print that every customer always reads, eh?

How To Get Clients

If you work at one of these major trading empires, chances are high that you will have clients simply handed to you. Whether they've been cast off from an old employee or they signed up online with your brokerage, the amount of people interested in investing will probably surprise you.

However, what should you do if you have to hunt down clients on your own?

1.) **Think of clients like wealthy patrons.** For example - The Smithsonian gets a new exhibit on the Titanic, so their marketing representatives contact all family members of the surviving passengers of the Titanic with the intent of earning donations through familiarity. Similarly, you can hunt down investors by acting like a stock market bloodhound. Do you have a particular client who likes to invest in beauty supplies? The next time a volatile, beauty-based penny stock pink sheet graces your desk, contact that client.

2.) **Don't skip office parties.** Jared is stressed and fighting with his wife, and he needs to unload some clients.

Rebecca knows that the historical society of downtown Dayton is wanting to invest in market shares, but she doesn't have the time to spend with a large group of investors. If you want to pick up clients through personal relationships, *(you do, because it's easy)*, then you need to stay buddy buddy with you coworkers.

3.) **Cold-call**. If you're apprehensive about speaking with strangers about their monetary situation, they you probably shouldn't be a stock broker. Gird your loins, knock on some doors, and call random names from a phone book.

4.) **Find a 'Potential Investors' list**. If your firm does not have a list of potential clients, then ask around. It's unlikely that a coworker would share information about potential investors with you, but there's no harm in trying!

Taking The Heat

The most difficult challenge you will face is dealing with **angry investors.**

No one is perfect and sometimes your choices will fail. Blame it on the bad economy or the companies that tanked...but whatever you do, learn to always show confidence.

As mentioned earlier...your ability to sell the idea of *"easy money"* is really what's being tested here.

If clients feel that they can trust you and that you will eventually lead them into the promised land of investments, then a few potholes along the way won't greatly disturb them.

The Road To Being A Broker

So, how do you become an investor? By doing exactly this:

- Build a diverse investment portfolio.
- Educate yourself *(formal or otherwise)*.
- Decide between the three types of brokers.

- Apply and get accepted into a firm.

- Take the two required standardized test *(Series 7 and 63)*.

- Build up a client base.

- Keep researching and learning EVERY DAY.

Chapter 7

Risking It All Over a Penny

The Nature Of Penny Stocks

"The idea that the odds of an event with a fixed probability increase or decrease depending on recent occurrences of the event is called the ***gambler's fallacy****. For example, if Kerrich landed, say, 44 heads in the first 100 tosses, the coin would not develop a bias towards the tails in order to catch up! That's what is at the root of such ideas as "her luck has run out" and "He is due." That does not happen. For what it's worth, a good streak doesn't jinx you, and a bad one, unfortunately , does not mean better luck is in store."* - **Leonard Mlodinow,** The Drunkard's Walk: How Randomness Rules Our Lives

To sum up, the *penny stock market is complex*. What has worked before should not be relied upon to work again. What was a disaster before should not be X'd off the list entirely.

Thus, beware this "**gambler's fallacy.**"

If you've invested in 16 failed companies in a row, that does now mean that you are bound to stumble on gold eventually. There is no room in the penny stock market for hope or luck, but there is room for *skepticism*.

Similarly, just because you've invested in avocados and lost money twice before does not mean that the avocado importation market can't skyrocket overnight.

If Dr. Phil suddenly started preaching the health benefits of avocados, all those tiny farms and shipping businesses would suddenly be a boon for any wise investor.

> *Then are investors like Timothy Sykes telling the truth when they insist that investing is a predictable science?*

While there are definitely patterns present in any stock market, it is extremely unwise to think that any investment you make is a sure bet. Not only is it unwise, but it's also not true. *Think about this* - large companies have entire departments dedicated to PR and stock management.

Penny stock companies have less resources and less funds, and therefore a higher chance to tank before anyone is the wiser. Fortunately, they also possess a stunningly beautiful ability to make millionaires out of the most unlikely investors.

- One day you could be flipping burgers and bussing tables...the next day you'll quit your job and never work another day in your life because your shares in a company like Red Bull have skyrocketed.

If this kind of *risk* and *potential for return* is something you'd like to wet your whistle with, then penny stock trading is perfect for you; and it can all be fun and exciting.

The Real Secret Weapon To Penny Stock Investing

What is truly the **secret** behind successful penny stock trading?

- You might think being wealthy to begin with is most important, while your friends might value being connected to the right investing resources or broker.

Yes, these things definitely help, but they are not the end-all be-all of investing. The secret is actually *not an outside resource* at all!

You brain. That inner organ that produces enough energy to power a light bulb and can process information as fast as 268 miles per hour...this is the ultimate resource for investing.

The name of the game is *common sense*, a *thirst for knowledge*, and *self-control.*

Have you heard the terms *"smart investing"* and *"save smart?"*

Notice <u>two important things</u> here - "**smart**" implies work on your part. "Smart" means doing the research and applying conceptual intelligence to every investing situation. And secondly, these phrases are intrinsic.

The advice is not *"choose a smart broker"* or *"smart stocks."* No, those things would suggest that you should rely on other people or companies for your financial providence. What the actual investing cliche's are saying is that...you have to go it alone intelligently.

Read or watch the news, get a grasp on the current economy, and understand supply and demand. These are the easy parts that you might even be doing already.

Task: How Far Can You Afford To Go?

Do an **accurate assessment** of your *own life* and *financial needs.*

If you can't anticipate what you're going to be doing as a consumer, you have no business guessing at what other people will be doing.

Use self-evaluation to assess exactly how much *"extra"* money you have for investing.

- This part is important because snapping back funds once you've put them out there is going to be too difficult to solve last-minute rent emergencies or broken car repairs.

With that out of the way, it's time to take a look at how much time you have to be playing around in the stock market.

- If you have a full-time job, family obligations, and time-consuming hobbies, then you might want to consider *finding a stock broker.*

- If you're retired or want investing to be a major "hobby" of yours, then by all means - go it alone!

Regardless how you approach investing in penny stocks, *in both instances*, you will still be doing some work.

Even if you hire a broker, you will still need to research your broker, know your own financial limitations, and decide how aggressive you want to be in the market.

The key to investing, then, is your **mental strength** and **motivation** to how successful you want to be.

"Mental strength is really important because you either win or lose in your mind. And I'm not solely talking about sporting matches, boxing events - anything you do, you do it first with your mental strength. And you can actually train and develop it, and I am responsible for what I'm saying because I have experience with that." - **Wladimir Klitschko**

Overview

Finding a broker:

- Decide how involved you want to be in the investing process.

- Choose three brokerage firms that match up with your wants and needs.

- Assess which one has the most manageable fees.

- Speak to a financial assistant at that firm about your goals.

- Specify what kind of stocks you want to go after *(low-to-high risk)*.

- Instruct them to start investing for you.

Investing in stocks yourself:

- Decide how risky you want to get *(are pink sheet stocks a go?)*.

- Download an investing program and set up your profile.

- Search stocks by type, value, and trade history.

- Buy shares in the most profitable-looking companies.
- Watch your portfolio like a hawk.
- Sell when appropriate.
- Repeat!

Resources:

Here are some resources to look at. (*Remember, if you're not experienced enough to know a "tip" from a "pump and dump scheme," then you need to stay away from *biased affiliated* newsletters and forums).

Brokers and Firms:

- Scottrade *(less options with less fees)*
- Fidelity *(more options, more fees, $2500 minimum to open an account)*
- Etrade *(charges an average amount in fees, asks for a $1000 minimum investing start)*
- Charles Schwab *(a pricier firm, but trusted name in investing)*

Penny Stocks Newsletters and Tips:

- otpicks.com *(slightly questionable website and outdated "picks." Use this to see what the people behind the curve are doing...and avoid their mistakes.)*

- wallstreetpennies.com *(decent stock alerts delivered to your email)*

- Twitter.com *(follow the companies you're invested in. If they have to release a PR statement about anything...it's probably time to sell.)*

- Reddit.com/r/pennystocks and Reddit.com/r/stocks

- Yahoo.com - Stock Market

Tools/Software (From the 2015 best software list)

- Telechart TC2000

- Trade Station

- E-signal
- Metastocks
- EquityFeed
- Ninja Trader
- Profit Source
- Echartar
- Vector Vest
- Elmwood Data

PERSONAL THANK YOU!

We can't thank you enough for entrusting in us to help you improve your life with our NO-To-KNOW Series.

We hope this has helped you, and you have gotten a ton of value.

If you can leave us a review on where you have purchased this book, we will be extremely appreciative in helping us improve the series.

Be sure to check other books in the NO-To-KNOW Series.

If you have a topic you like for the series, be sure to let us know, as well as we always love your feedback.

Thank you!

- All of us here at NO-To-KNOW Publication

www.ingramcontent.com/pod-product-compliance
Lightning Source LLC
Chambersburg PA
CBHW030702190526
45164CB00004B/290

* 9 7 8 1 5 1 7 7 1 7 9 6 4 *